PAINT BY STICKER®

KIDS

PETS

workman

· NEW YORK ·

D1518004

Library of Congress Cataloging-in-Publication Data is available.

ISBN 978-1-5235-1936-1

Design by Terri Ruffino and Andrew Wang

The 10 low-poly images in this book are based on illustrations by Liam Brazier.

Workman books are available at special discounts when purchased in bulk for premiums and sales promotions as well as for fundraising or educational use. Special editions or book excerpts can also be created to specification. For details, please contact special.markets@hbgusa.com.

Workman Publishing Co., Inc., a subsidiary of Hachette Book Group, Inc.
1290 Avenue of the Americas
New York, NY 10104

workman.com

Distributed in Europe by Hachette Livre, 58 rue Jean Bleuzen, 92 178 Vanves Cedex, France.
Distributed in the United Kingdom by Hachette Book Group, UK, Carmelite House, 50 Victoria Embankment, London EC4Y 0DZ.

WORKMAN and PAINT BY STICKER are registered trademarks of Workman Publishing Co., Inc., a subsidiary of Hachette Book Group, Inc.

Printed in China

First printing May 2023

10 9 8 7 6 5 4 3 2 1

HOW TO PAINT BY STICKER

STICKER MAP

STICKER SHEET

53

1. PICK YOUR IMAGE.
Sticker maps for each image are in the front of the book. Do you want to sticker a fluffy bunny, or some colorful frogs? It's up to you!

2. FIND YOUR STICKERS.
Sticker sheets for each image are in the back of the book. Use the picture in the top right corner of each sticker sheet to find the one that goes with your image. Both the sticker sheet and the sticker map can be torn out of the book, so you don't have to flip back and forth between them.

3. MATCH THE NUMBERS.
Each sticker has a number that matches a space on the sticker map. Place each sticker in the space on the sticker map with the matching number. Be careful! The stickers aren't removable.

4. WATCH YOUR PAINTING COME TO LIFE!
After you've finished your masterpiece, you can frame it, use it as decoration, or give it as a gift.

ARE YOU READY? LET'S START STICKERING!

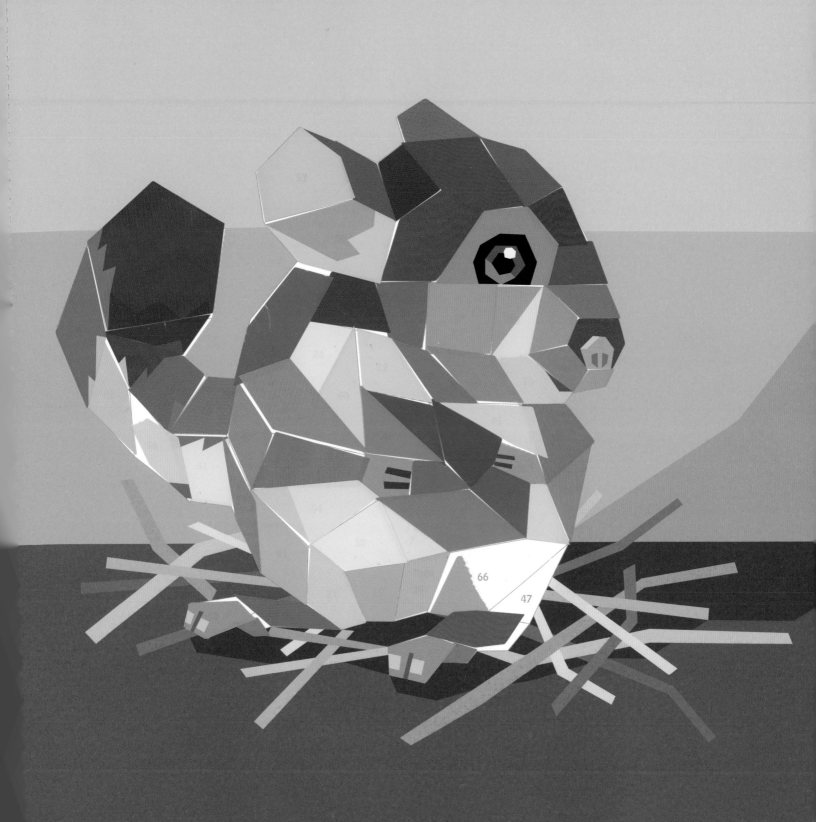

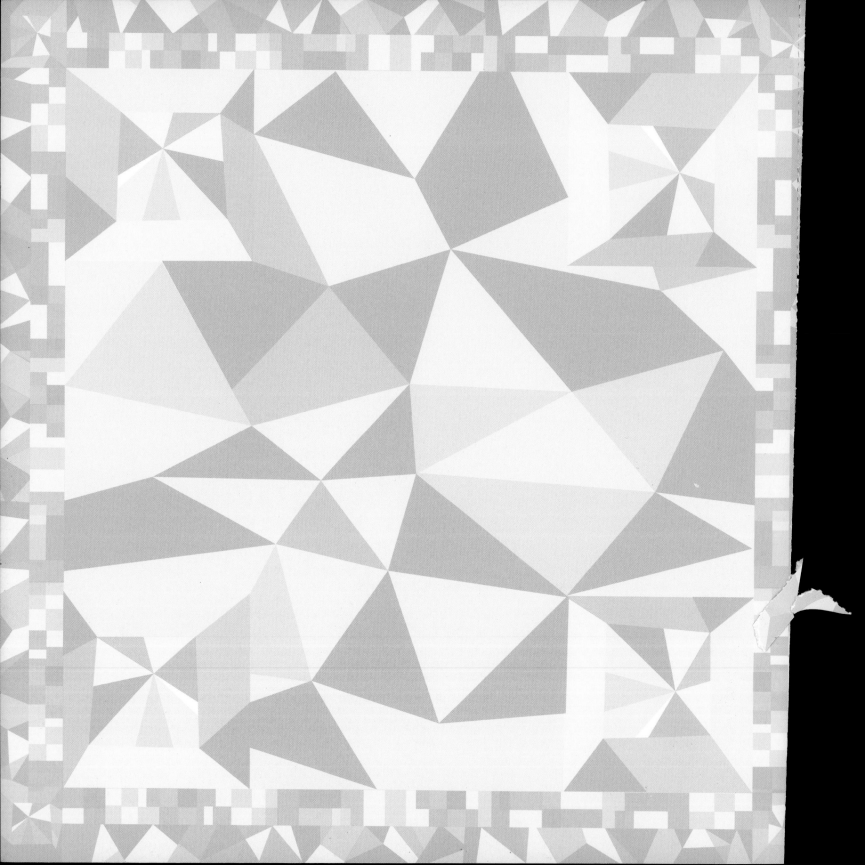

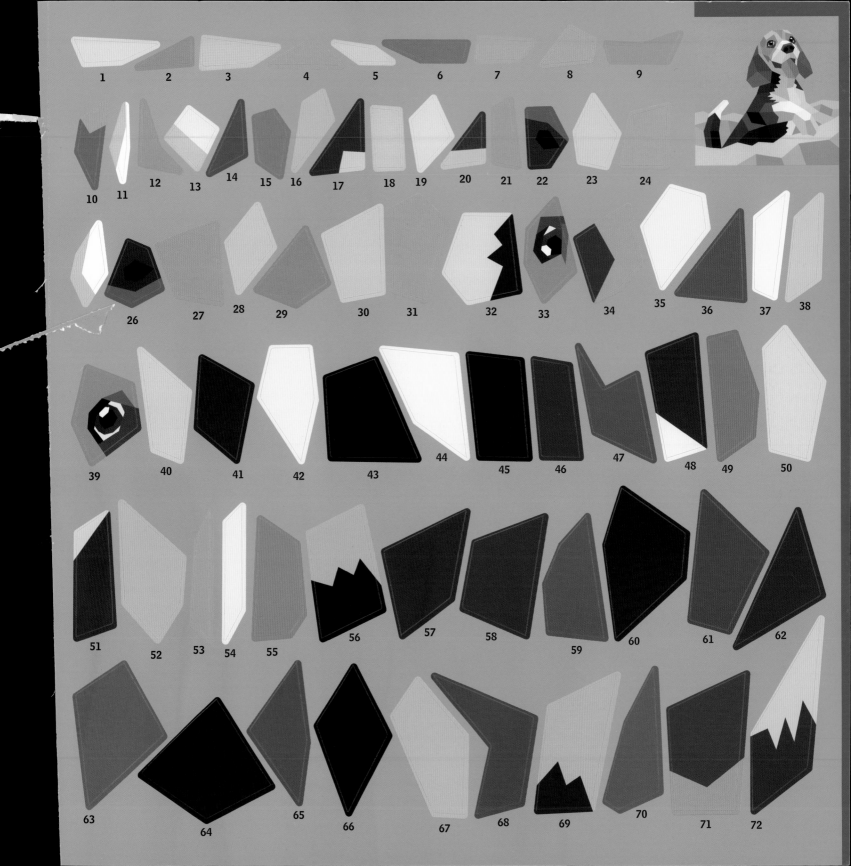

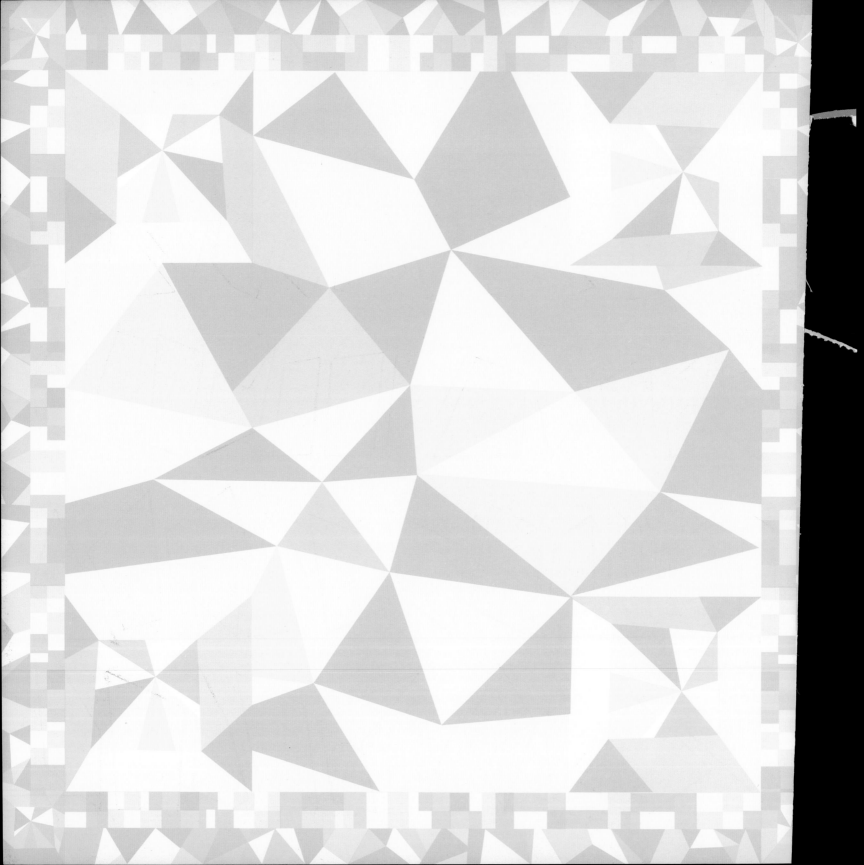

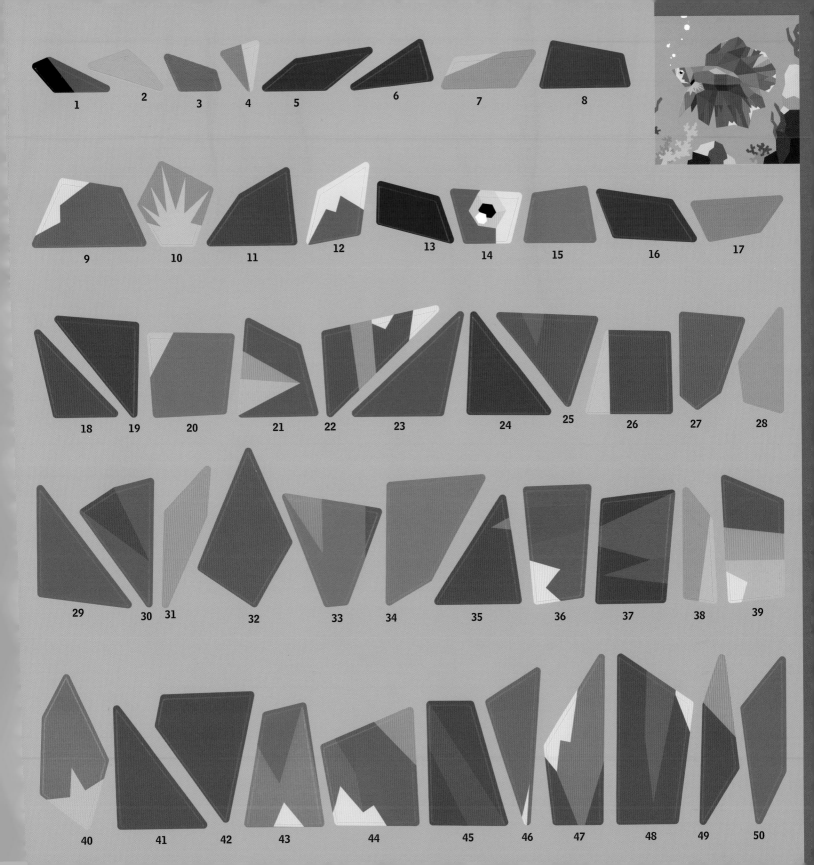

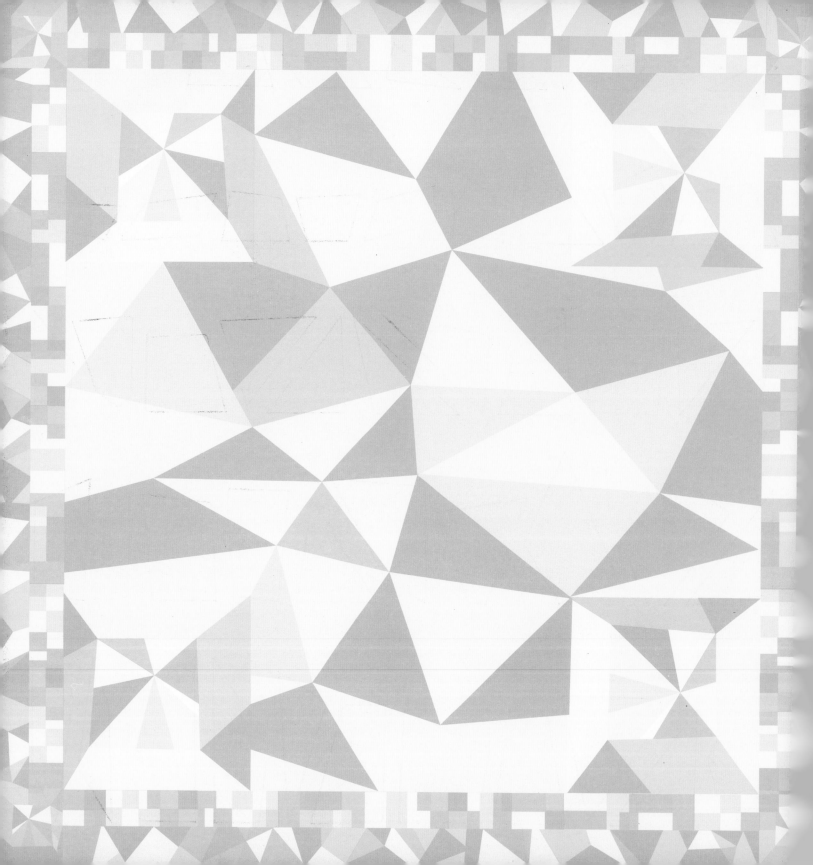

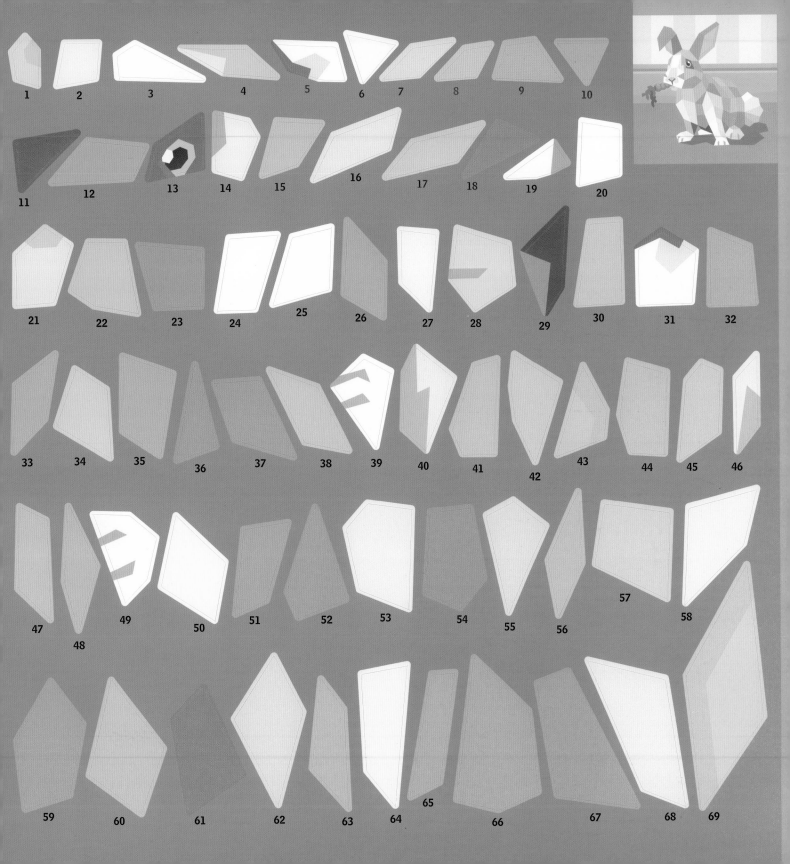

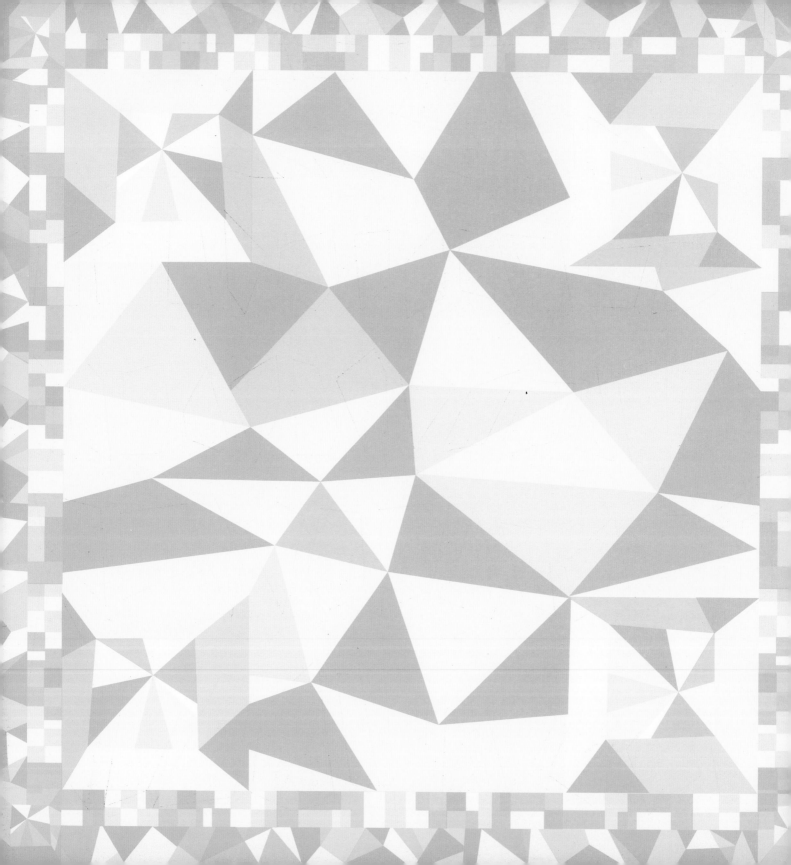

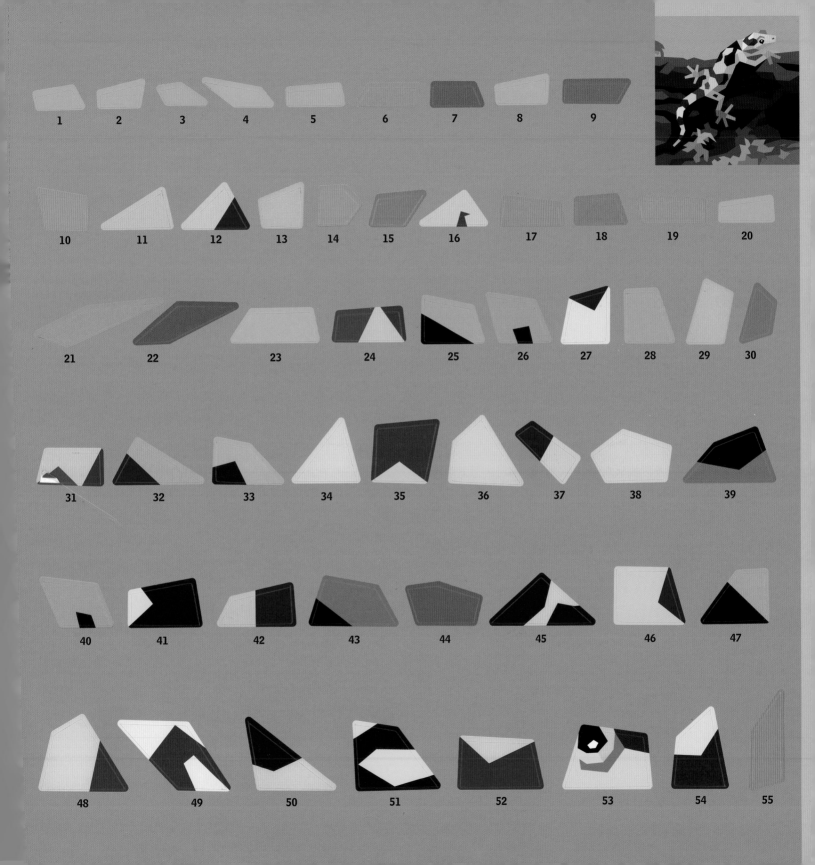

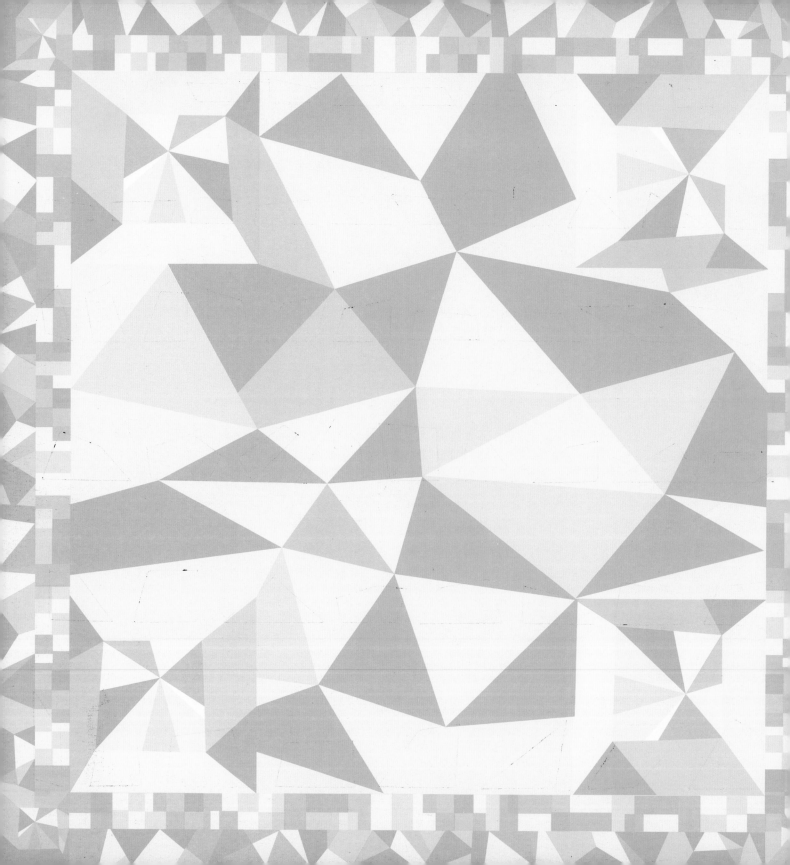

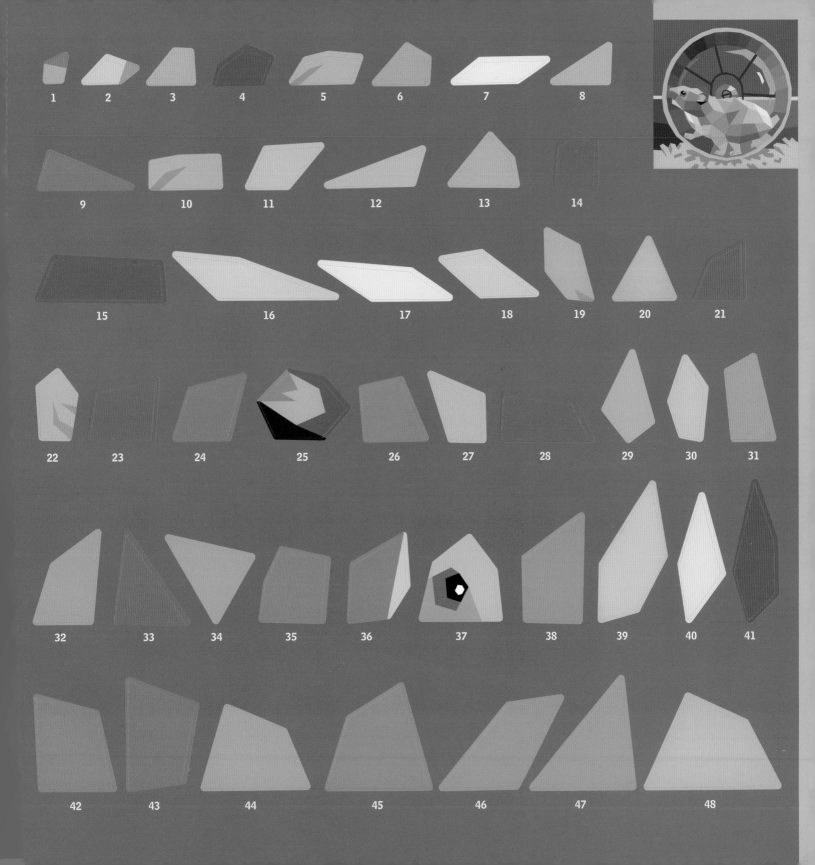

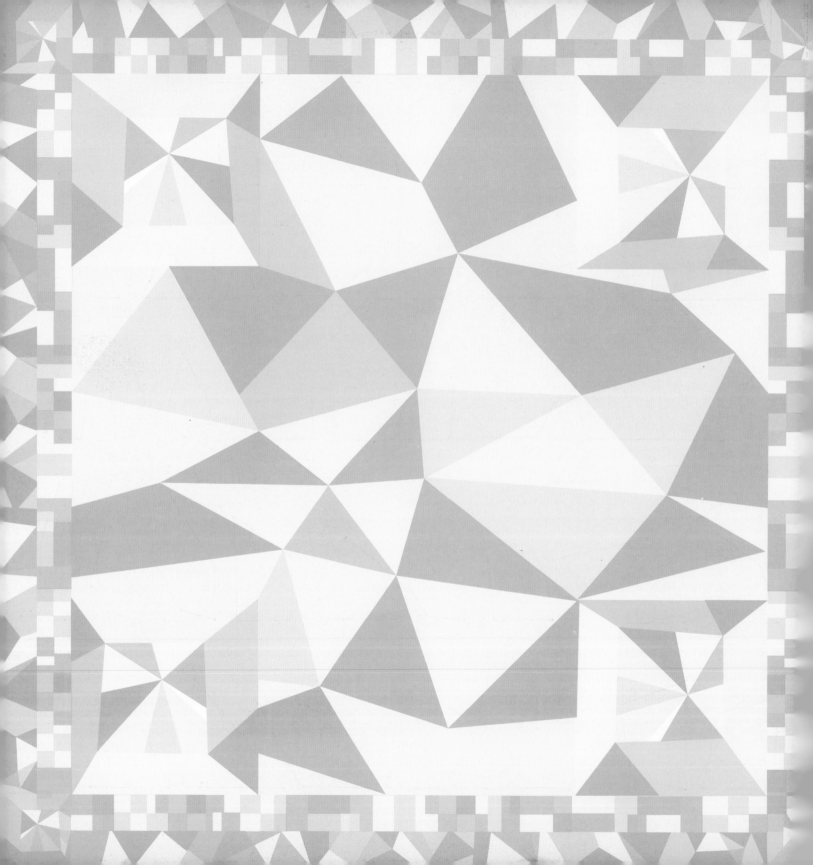

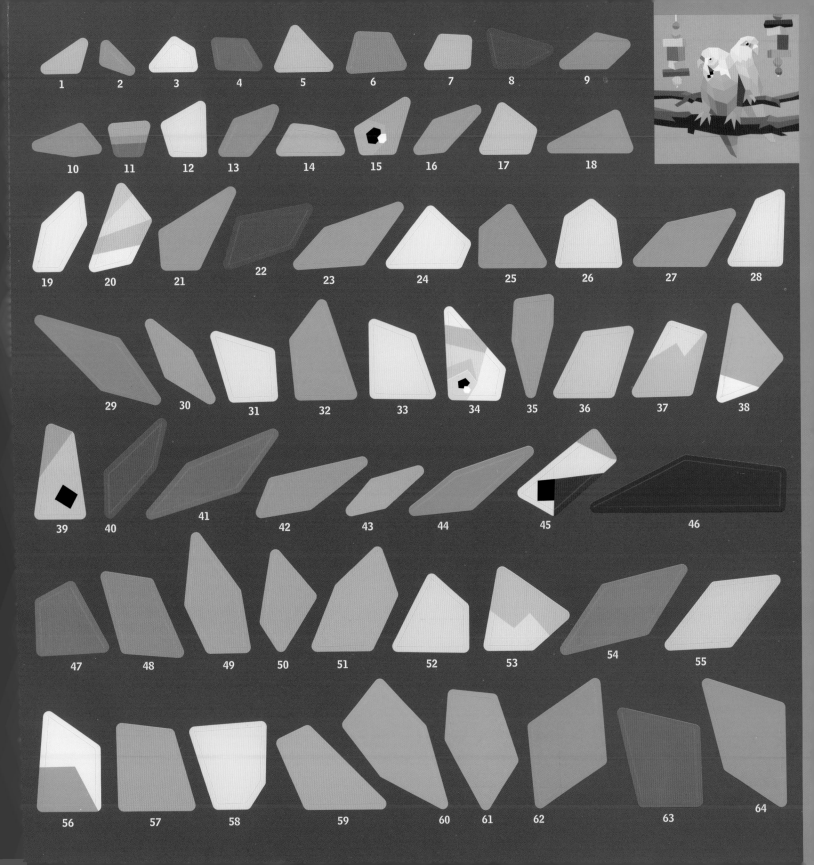

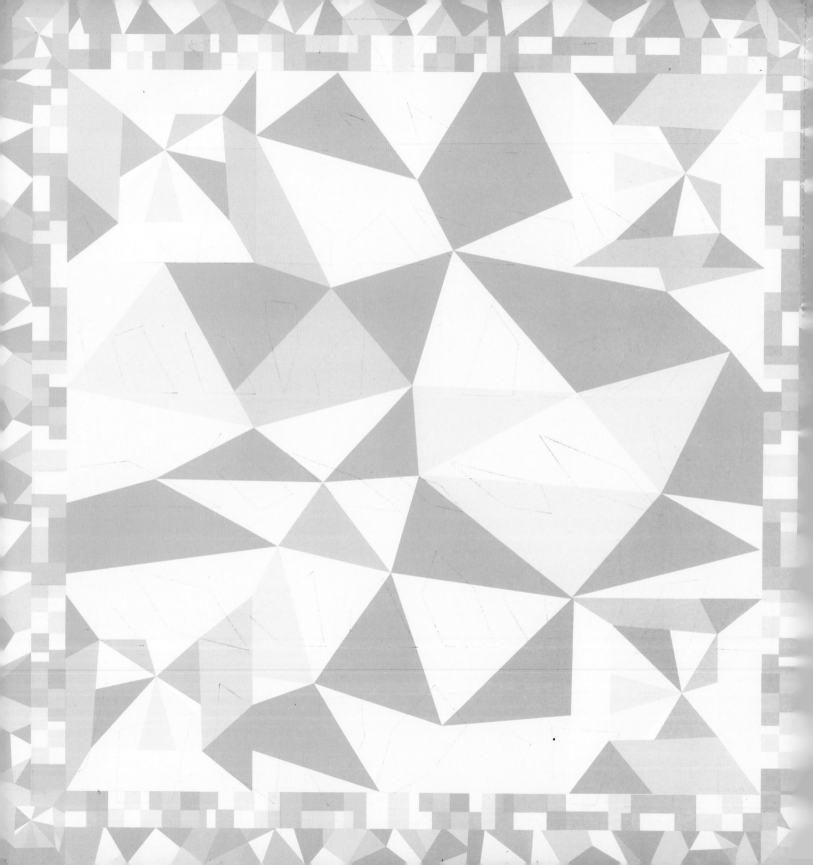